What's My Style?

I love creating elaborate patterns packed with detail so I can do lots of intricate coloring. I try to use as many colors as possible. Then I layer on lots of fun details. Here are some more examples of my work.

My studio is filled with natural light, tons of coloring supplies, and lots of inspiration, all of which motivate me to create and color!

Where to Start

You might find putting color on a fresh page stressful. It's okay! Here are a few tricks I use to get the ink flowing.

Start with an easy decision. If a design has leaves, without a doubt, that's where I start. No matter how wacky and colorful everything else gets, I always color the leaves in my illustrations green. I have no reason for it; it's just how it is! Try to find something in the design to help ground you by making an easy color decision: leaves are green, the sky is blue, etc.

Get inspired. Take a good look at everything in the illustration. You chose to color it for a reason. One little piece that you love will jump out and say, "Color me! Use red, please!" Or maybe it will say blue, or pink, or green. Just relax—it will let you know.

Follow your instincts. What colors do you love? Are you a big fan of purple? Or maybe yellow is your favorite. If you love it, use it!

Just go for it. Close your eyes, pick up a color, point to a spot on the illustration, and start! Sometimes starting is the hardest part, but it's the fastest way to finish!

Helpful Hints

There is no right or wrong. All colors work together, so don't be scared to mix it up. The results can be surprising!

Try it. Test your chosen colors on scrap paper before you start coloring your design. You can also test blending techniques and how to use different shapes and patterns for detail work—you can see how different media will blend with or show up on top of your chosen colors. I even use the paper to clean my markers or pens if necessary.

Make a color chart. A color chart is like a test paper for every single color you have! It provides a more accurate way to choose colors than selecting them based on the color of the marker's cap. To make a color chart, color a swatch with each marker, colored pencil, gel pen, etc. Label each swatch with the name or number of the marker so you can easily find it later.

Do you like warm colors?

How about cool colors?

Maybe you like warm and cool colors together!

Keep going. Even if you think you've ruined a piece, work through it. I go through the same cycle with my coloring: I love a piece at the beginning, and by the halfway point I nearly always dislike it. Sometimes by the end I love it again, and sometimes I don't, and that's okay. It's important to remember that you're coloring for you—no one else. If you really don't like a piece at the end, stash it away and remember that you learned something. You know what not to do next time. My studio drawers are full of everything from duds to masterpieces!

Be patient. Let markers, gel pens, and paints dry thoroughly between each layer. There's nothing worse than smudging a cluster of freshly inked dots across the page with your hand. Just give them a minute to dry and then you can move on to the next layer.

Use caution. Juicy/inky markers can "spit" when you uncap them. Open them away from your art piece.

Work from light to dark. It's much easier to make something darker gradually than to lighten it.

Shade with gray. A mid-tone lavender-gray marker is perfect for adding shadows to your artwork, giving it depth and making it pop right off the page!

Try blending fluid. If you like working with alcohol-based markers, a refillable bottle of blending fluid or a blending pen is a great investment. Aside from enabling you to easily blend colors together, it can help clean up unwanted splatters or mistakes—it may not take some colors away completely, but it will certainly lighten them. I use it to clean the body of my markers as I'm constantly smudging them with inky fingers. When a marker is running out of ink, I find adding a few drops of blending fluid to the ink barrel will make it last a bit longer.

Layering and Blending

I love layering and blending colors. It's a great way to create shading and give your finished piece lots of depth and dimension. The trick is to work from the lightest color to the darkest and then go over everything again with the lightest shade to keep the color smooth and bring all the layers together.

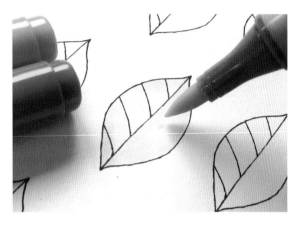

1 Apply a base layer with the lightest color.

2 Add the middle color, using it to create shading.

3 Smooth out the color by going over everything with the lightest color.

4 Add the darkest color, giving your shading even more depth. Use the middle color to go over the same area you colored in Step 2.

5 Go over everything with the lightest color as you did in Step 3.

Patterning and Details

Layering and blending will give your coloring depth and dimension. Adding patterning and details will really bring it to life. If you're not convinced, try adding a few details to one of your colored pieces with a white gel pen—that baby will make magic happen! Have fun adding all of the dots, doodles, and swirls you can imagine.

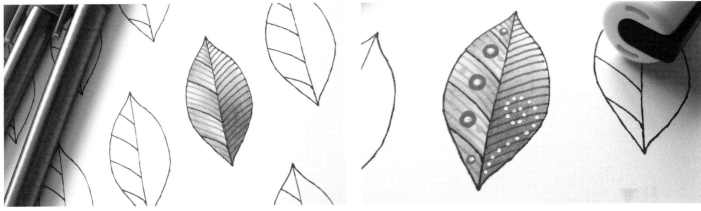

1 Once you've finished your coloring, blending, and layering, go back and add simple patterning like lines or dots. You can add your patterns in black or color. For this leaf, I used two different shades of green pen.

2 Now it's time to add some fun details using paint pens or gel pens. Here I used white, yellow, and more green.

This design really pops with lots of patterning and little details.

Coloring Supplies

I'm always asked about the mediums I use to color my illustrations. The answer would be really long if I listed every single thing, so here are a few of my favorites. Keep in mind that these are *my* favorites. When you color, you should use YOUR favorites!

Alcohol-based markers. I have many, and a variety of brands. My favorites have a brush nib—it's so versatile. A brush nib is perfect for tiny, tight corners, but is also able to cover a large, open space easily. I find I rarely get streaking, and if I do, it's usually because the ink is running low!

Fine-tip pens. Just like with markers, I have lots of different pens. I use them for my layers of detail work and for the itsy bitsy spots my markers can't get into.

Paint pens. These are wonderful! Because the ink is usually opaque, they stand out really well against a dark base color. I use extra fine point pens for their precision. Some paint pens are water based, so I can use a brush to blend the colors and create a cool watercolor effect.

Gel pens. I have a few, but I usually stick to white and neon colors that will stand out on top of dark base colors or other mediums.

Hello Angel #1401 Waves of Wings: marker pens, fineliner pens, paint pens

Hello Angel #1402 Eye of Nature: marker pens, fineliner pens, paint pens

Hello Angel #1404 On the Fly: watercolors, markers, fineliner pens, paint pens

Hello Angel #1407 Happy Hummingbird: markers, fineliner pens, paint pens

Hello Angel #1408 Radiant Flower: watercolors, marker pens, fineliner pens, paint pens

Hello Angel #1425 Maple: marker pens, fineliner pens, paint pens

Hello Angel #1426 All the Buzz: markers, fineliner pens, paint pens

Hello Angel #1429 Lucky Ladybug: watercolors, markers, fineliner pens, paint pens

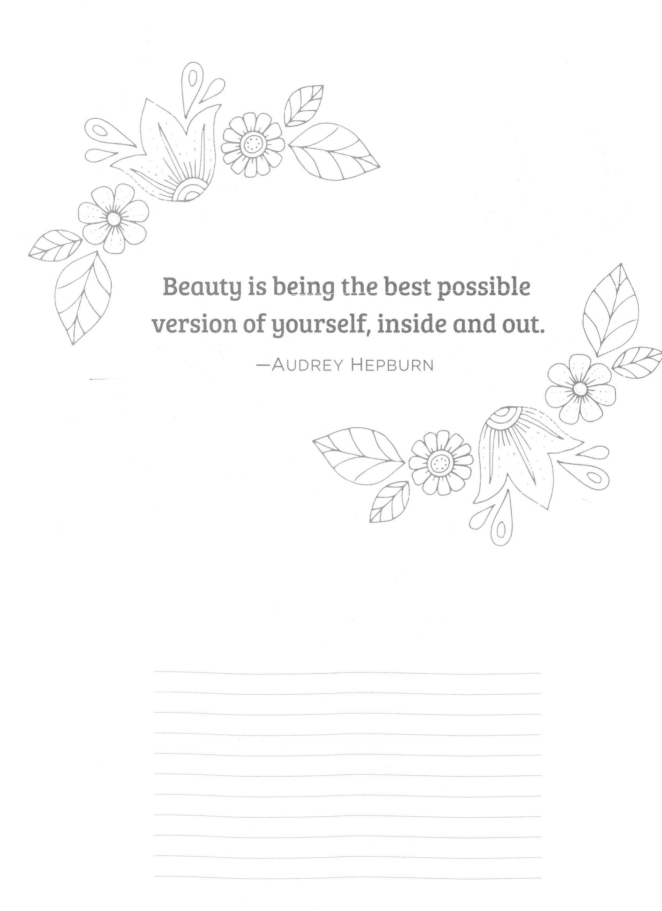

Beauty is being the best possible version of yourself, inside and out.

—Audrey Hepburn

Don't judge each day
by the harvest you reap but by
the seeds that you plant.

—ROBERT LOUIS STEVENSON

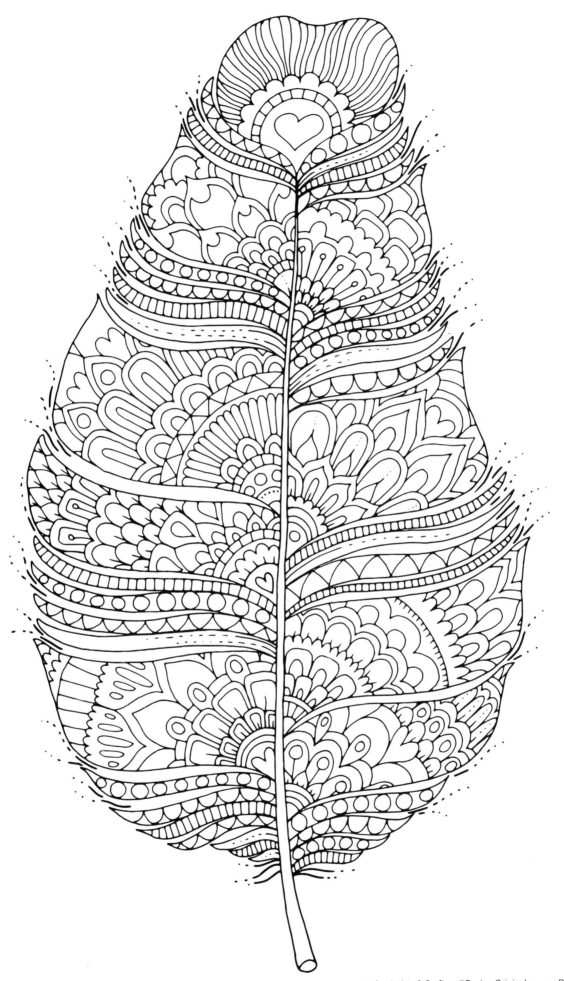

Success is not final, failure is not fatal:
it is the courage to continue that counts.

—Unknown

Time is a dressmaker
specializing in alterations.

—FAITH BALDWIN

Yesterday is not ours to recover,
but tomorrow is ours to win or lose.

—Lyndon B. Johnson

_____

_____

_____

_____

_____

_____

_____

_____

_____

_____

There were no violins or warning bells . . .
no sense that my little life
was about to change.
But we never know, do we?
Life turns on a dime.

—STEPHEN KING, *11/22/63*

The desire for symmetry, for balance,
for rhythm in form as well as in sound,
is one of the most inveterate
of human instincts.

—EDITH WHARTON

If you want to lead an extraordinary life,
find out what the ordinary do—and don't do it.

—Tommy Newberry

_____

_____

_____

_____

_____

_____

_____

_____

_____

_____

Nothing that is can pause or stay;
The moon will wax, the moon will wane,
The mist and cloud will turn to rain,
The rain to mist and cloud again,
To-morrow be to-day.

—HENRY WADSWORTH LONGFELLOW

He who is not courageous enough
to take risks will accomplish nothing in life.

—Muhammad Ali

Continuity gives us roots; change gives us branches, letting us stretch and grow and reach new heights.

—PAULINE R. KEZER

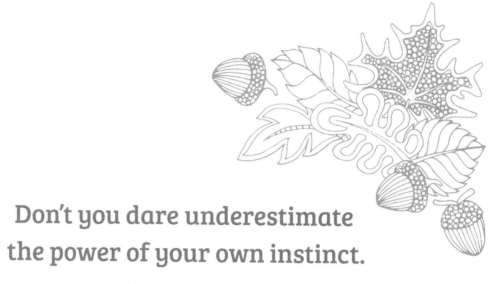

Don't you dare underestimate
the power of your own instinct.

—BARBARA CORCORAN

All my life through, the new sights of Nature made me rejoice like a child.

—MARIE CURIE

_____

_____

_____

_____

_____

_____

_____

_____

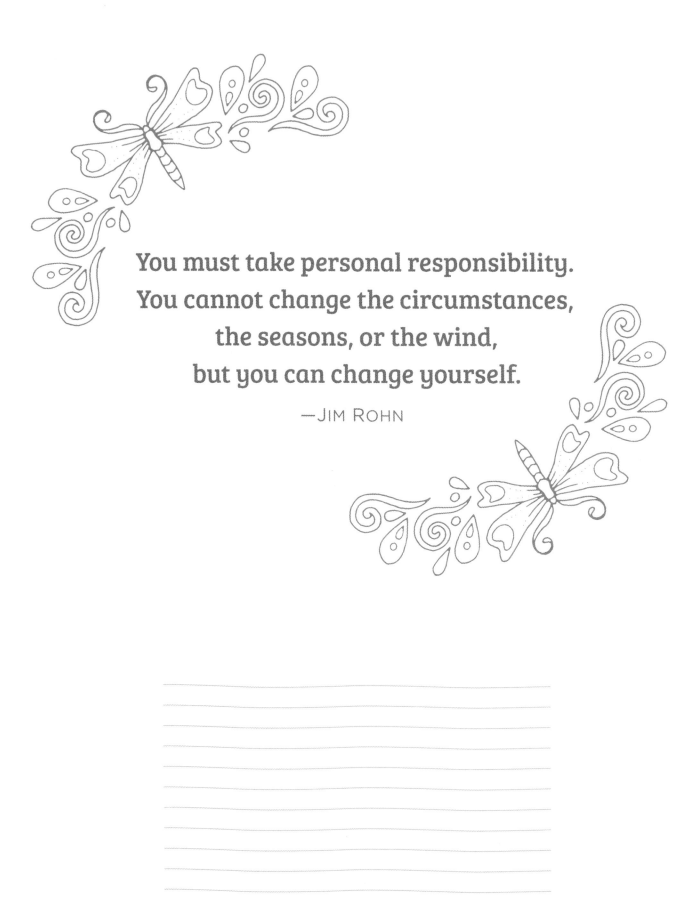

You must take personal responsibility.
You cannot change the circumstances,
the seasons, or the wind,
but you can change yourself.

—JIM ROHN

Shared joy is a double joy;
shared sorrow is half a sorrow.

—SWEDISH PROVERB

_____
_____
_____
_____
_____
_____
_____
_____

Once you choose hope, anything's possible.

—CHRISTOPHER REEVE

With this design, take the time to get to know different hues of one color—blue, for instance.

A thing of beauty is a joy for ever.

—JOHN KEATS, *ENDYMION*

Hello Angel #1401 Waves and Wings

Use your own eye color as inspiration and make this a creative self-portrait!

To acquire knowledge, one must study;
but to acquire wisdom, one must observe.

—MARILYN VOS SAVANT

Hello Angel #1402 Eye of Nature

Butterflies are so naturally colorful that you may want to let your background sit back and let them shine.

Every single thing changes and is
changing always in this world.
Yet with the same light the moon goes on shining.

—SAIGYO

Hello Angel #1403 Grand Specimen

By blending colors you can make the wavy background seem to move. See how the pink and purple play off each other?

I always did something I was a little
not ready to do. I think that's how you grow.

—MARISSA MAYER

A bold, red heart amplifies this bit of zen wisdom.

There is only one time that is important—
now! It is the most important time because it is
the only time when we have any power.

—LEO TOLSTOY

Need some inspiration? Take a walk through the woods and see how many shades of green and brown you can find!

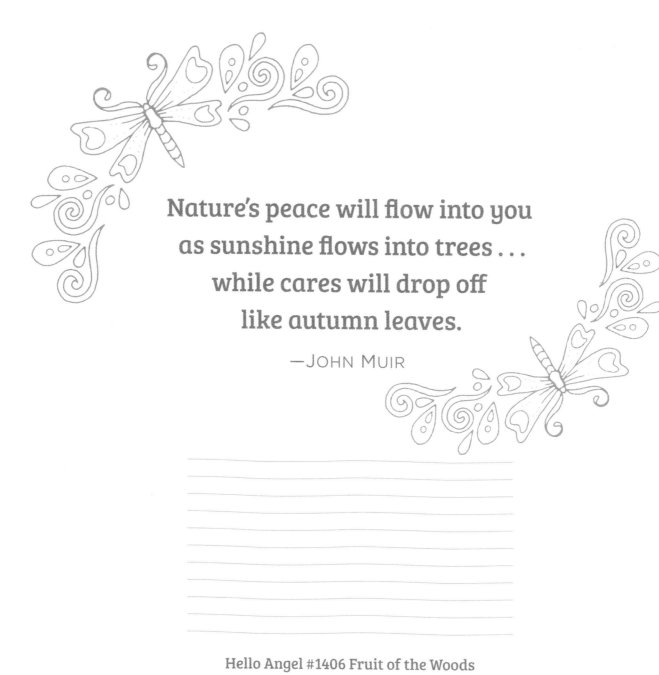

Nature's peace will flow into you
as sunshine flows into trees . . .
while cares will drop off
like autumn leaves.

—JOHN MUIR

Hello Angel #1406 Fruit of the Woods

How wonderful is the sight of a hummingbird getting its nectary lunch from a blooming flower? Use happy, bright colors.

Everything you can imagine is real.

—PABLO PICASSO

Hello Angel #1407 Happy Hummingbird

Since there are so many repeating shapes,
your color choices can make a huge difference in
determining how the eye moves across this design!

The most important thing in life is to
learn how to give out love, and to let it come in.

—MORRIE SCHWARTZ

_____

_____

_____

_____

_____

_____

_____

_____

_____

Hello Angel #1408 Radiant Flower

They must often change,
who would be constant
in happiness or wisdom.

—CONFUCIUS

In all things of nature
there is something of the marvelous.

—ARISTOTLE

_____
_____
_____
_____
_____
_____
_____
_____
_____
_____

Relation is the essence of everything that exists.

—MEISTER ECKHART

I take pleasure in my transformations.
I look quiet and consistent, but few know
how many women there are in me.

—ANAÏS NIN

The mind is just like a muscle—the more you exercise it, the stronger it gets and the more it can expand.

—IDOWU KOYENIKAN

When the winds of change blow,
some people build walls
and others build windmills.

—CHINESE PROVERB

The most beautiful people I've known are those who have known trials, have known struggles, have known loss, and have found their way out of the depths.

—Elisabeth Kübler-Ross

To live is the rarest thing in the world. Most people exist, that is all.

—Oscar Wilde

Among life's precious jewels,
Genuine and rare,
The one that we call friendship
Has worth beyond compare.

—UNKNOWN

Never doubt that a small group of thoughtful, committed citizens can change the world; indeed, it is the only thing that ever has.

—MARGARET MEAD

The birds are molting. If only man could molt also—
his mind once a year its errors,
his heart once a year its useless passions.

—James Allen

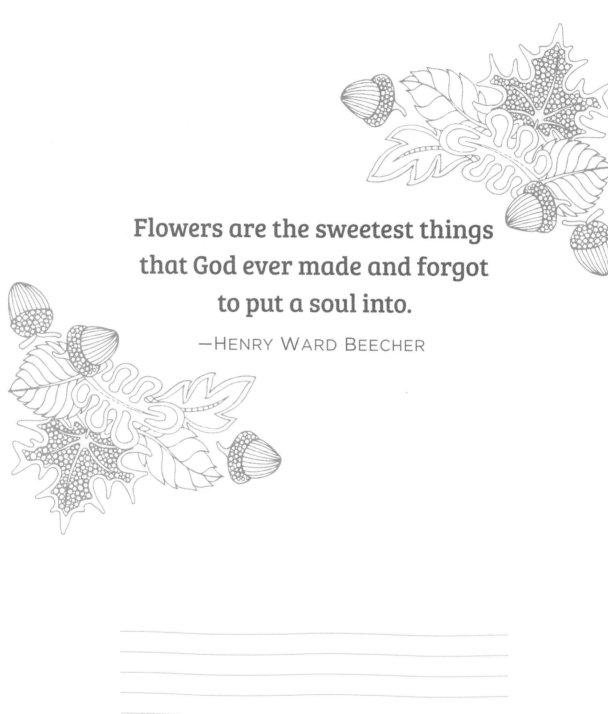

Flowers are the sweetest things
that God ever made and forgot
to put a soul into.

—Henry Ward Beecher

No man is an island, entire of itself;
every man is a piece of the continent,
a part of the main.

—JOHN DONNE

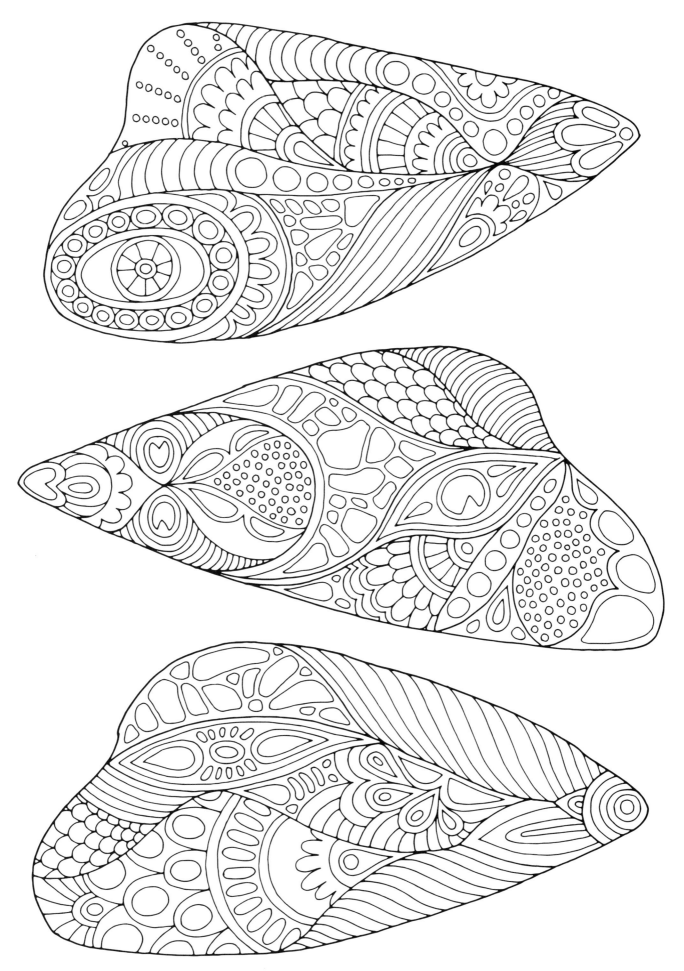

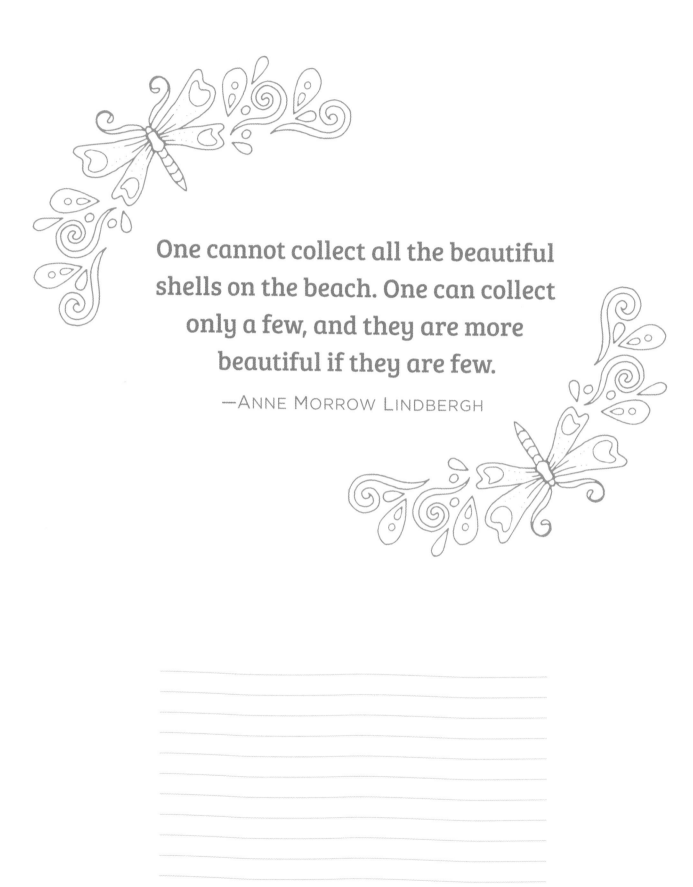

One cannot collect all the beautiful shells on the beach. One can collect only a few, and they are more beautiful if they are few.

—ANNE MORROW LINDBERGH

To finish the moment, to find the journey's end in every step of the road, to live the greatest number of good hours, is wisdom.

—RALPH WALDO EMERSON, "EXPERIENCE"

I believe the world is incomprehensibly beautiful—
an endless prospect of magic and wonder.

—Ansel Adams

Dots, loops, arches, triangles—this design has patterning for days!
What will be your system for filling them in?

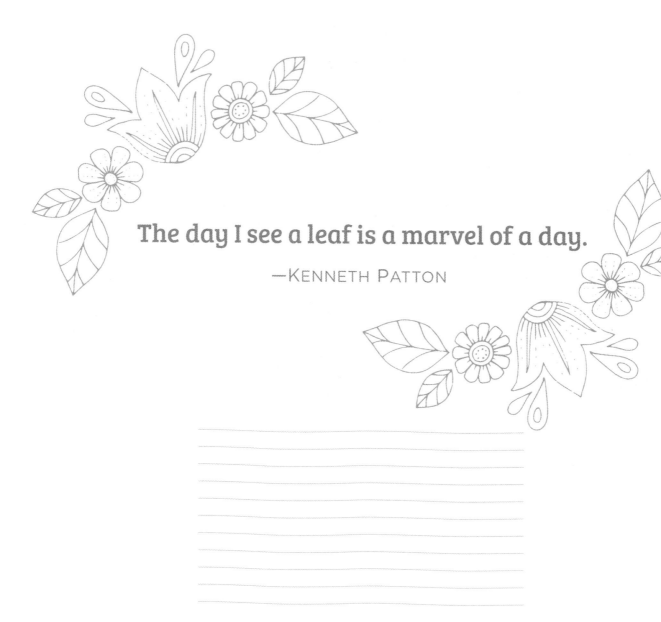

The day I see a leaf is a marvel of a day.

—KENNETH PATTON

_____
_____
_____
_____
_____
_____
_____
_____
_____

Hello Angel #1425 Maple

The empty white space on the bees' thoraxes makes for an intriguing pattern opportunity—can you think of something interesting?

The way to get started is to quit talking and begin doing.

—WALT DISNEY

Hello Angel #1426 All the Buzz

Try a soft-toned palette for some
colored pencil-fueled mandala meditation!

One ought, every day at least, to hear a little song,
read a good poem, see a fine picture,
and, if it were possible, to speak
a few reasonable words.

—JOHANN WOLFGANG VON GOETHE

Hello Angel #1427 Rolling Mandalas

©Hello Angel, www.helloangelcreative.com. From *Hello Angel Beauty of Nature Expanded Design Collection for Artists & Crafters* ©Design Originals, www.D-Originals.com

Spend time coming up with a scintillating color scheme and your result may be as beautiful as the example!

How wonderful it is that nobody
need wait a single moment before
starting to improve the world.

—ANNE FRANK

Hello Angel #1428 Hex Sign

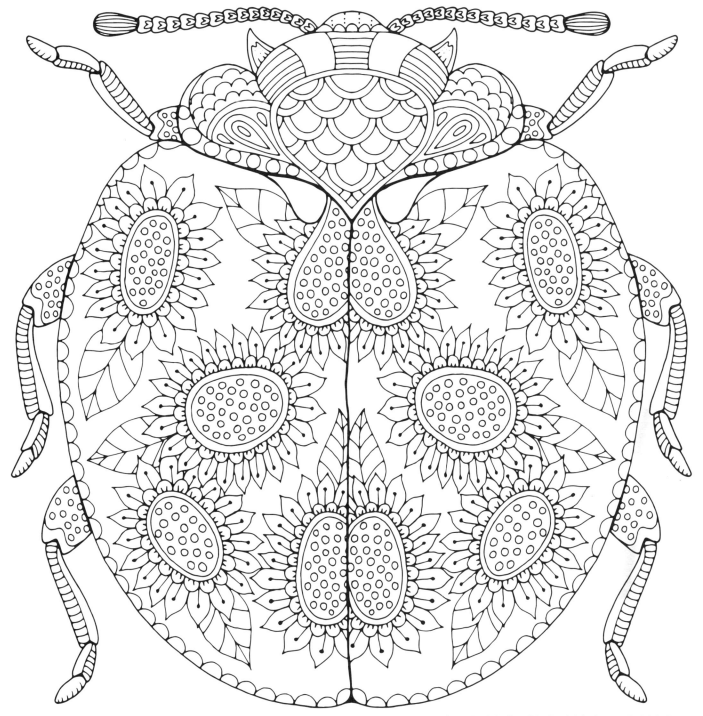

Symmetry in a design is something you can either reinforce
or de-emphasize with your coloring choices.

You can go as far as your mind lets you.
What you believe, remember, you can achieve.

—MARY KAY ASH

Hello Angel #1429 Lucky Ladybug

The heavy yellow, or goldenrod, adds deep texture to this buggy, wingy scene. See if you can replicate the idea.

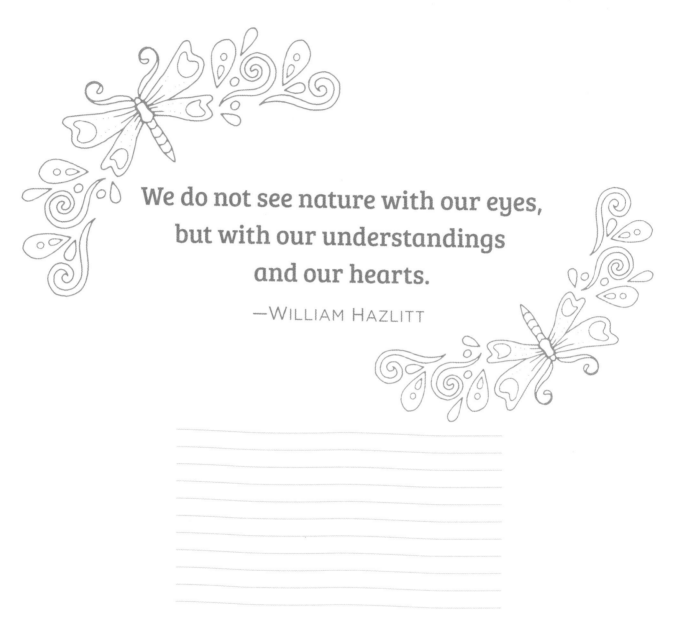

We do not see nature with our eyes,
but with our understandings
and our hearts.

—WILLIAM HAZLITT

Hello Angel #1430 Cooperation

When you put almost all the colors of the color wheel in play,
the outcome can be stunning!

Growth is the only evidence of life.

—JOHN HENRY NEWMAN

Hello Angel #1431 Perfection

These fluttering beauties have found the perfect spot.
Make them and their surroundings as vivid as you can!

May the wings of the butterfly kiss the sun
And find your shoulder to light on,
To bring you luck, happiness, and riches
Today, tomorrow, and beyond.

—IRISH BLESSING

_____
_____
_____
_____
_____
_____
_____
_____
_____

Hello Angel #1432 Verdant Garden

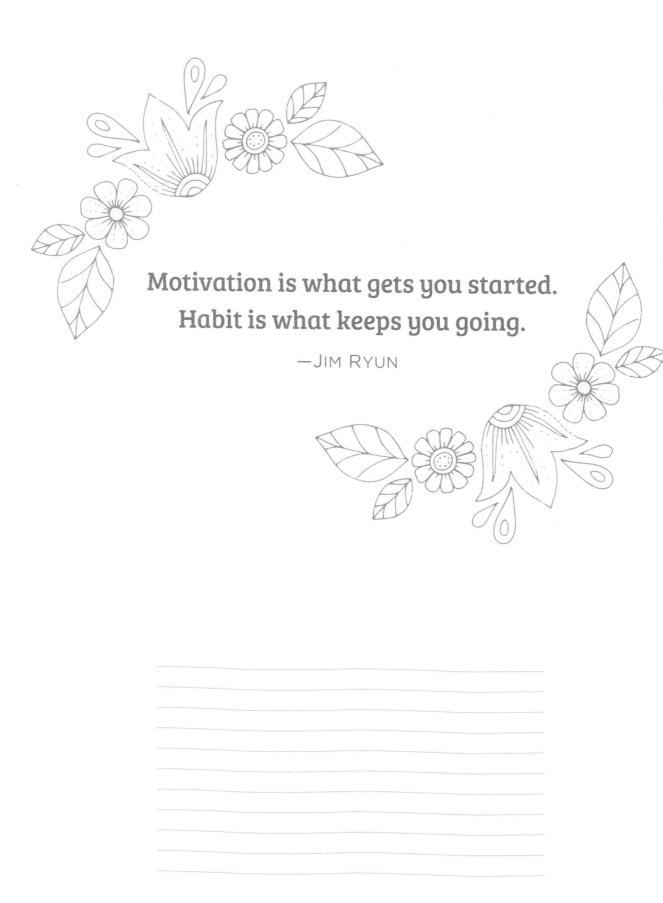

Motivation is what gets you started.
Habit is what keeps you going.

—JIM RYUN

All the art of living lies in a fine
mingling of letting go and holding on.

—Havelock Ellis

Life moves forward. The old leaves wither, die and fall away, and the new growth extends forward into the light.

—BRYANT MCGILL

I would not waste my life in friction
when it could be turned into momentum.

—FRANCES WILLARD

The golden way is to be friends with the world and to regard the whole human family as one.

—Mahatma Gandhi

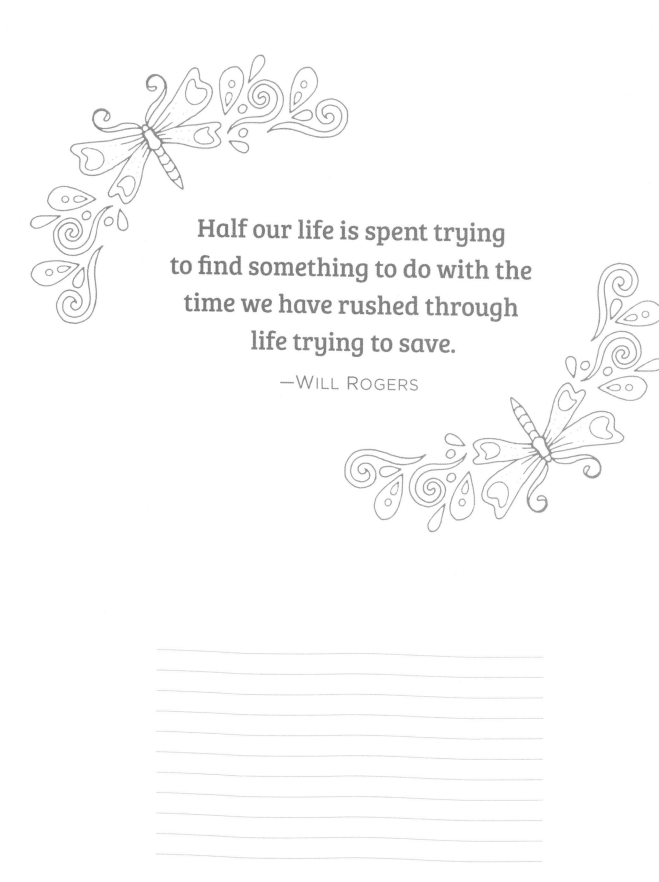

Half our life is spent trying
to find something to do with the
time we have rushed through
life trying to save.

—WILL ROGERS

If you want to increase your success rate,
double your failure rate.

—THOMAS WATSON

_____

_____

_____

_____

_____

_____

_____

_____

_____

I felt my lungs inflate with the onrush of scenery—
air, mountains, trees, people. I thought,
"This is what it is to be happy."

—SYLVIA PLATH

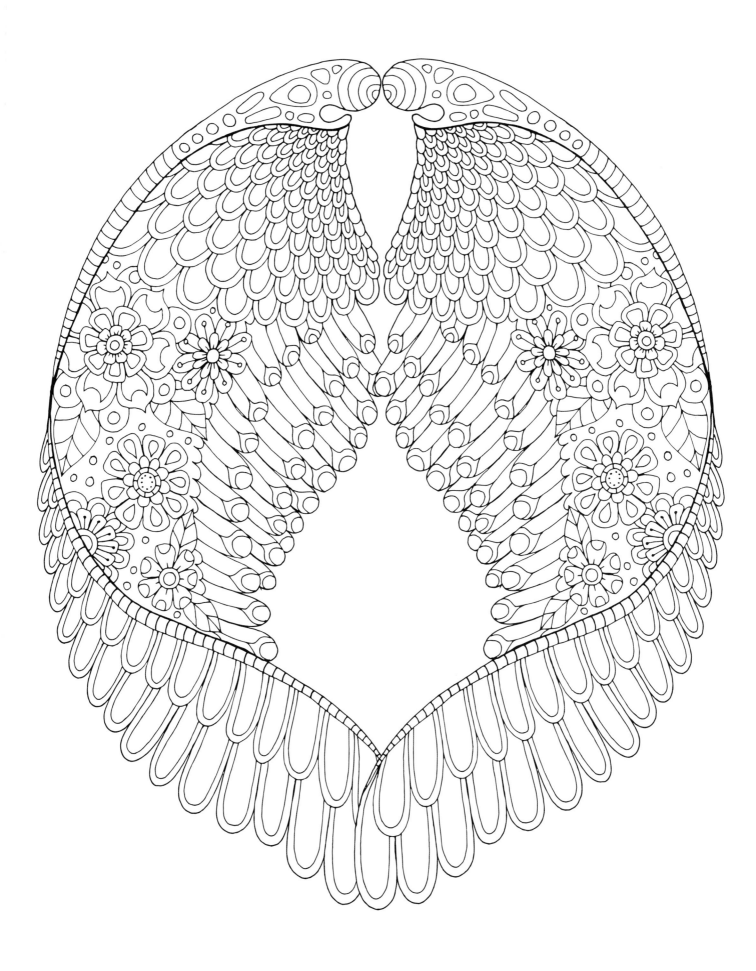

**Tough times never last,
but tough people do.**

—ROBERT H. SCHULLER

There are two ways of exerting one's strength: one is pushing down, the other is pulling up.

—Booker T. Washington

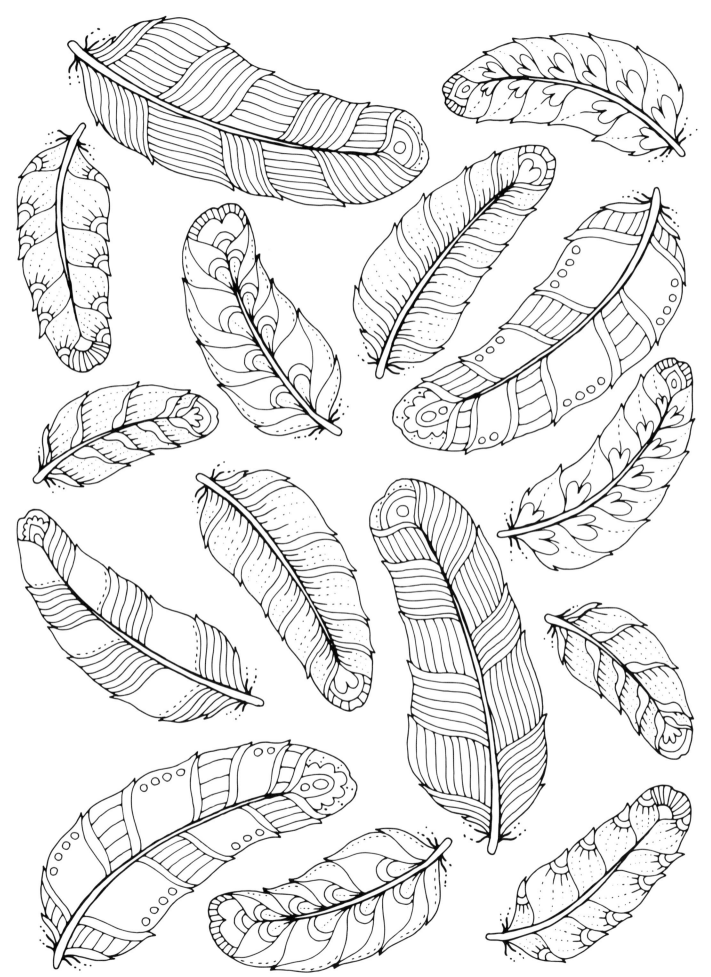

Life has many ways of testing a person's will,
either by having nothing happen at all or by
having everything happen all at once.

—PAULO COELHO

If you don't like something, change it.
If you can't change it, change your attitude.

—MAYA ANGELOU

_____
_____
_____
_____
_____
_____
_____
_____
_____

If you surrender to the wind, you can ride it.

—TONI MORRISON

_____
_____
_____
_____
_____
_____
_____
_____
_____
_____

I've come to believe that each
of us has a personal calling that's
as unique as a fingerprint.

—OPRAH WINFREY

The poetry of earth is never dead.

—JOHN KEATS

Hope is the thing with feathers
That perches in the soul,
And sings the tune without the words,
And never stops at all....

—EMILY DICKINSON

_____
_____
_____
_____
_____
_____
_____
_____
_____